EDGE BOOKS™

NASCAR RACING

Richard Petty

by A. R. Schaefer

Consultant:
Suzanne Wise, Librarian
Stock Car Racing Collection, Belk Library
Appalachian State University
Boone, North Carolina

Capstone
press®

Mankato, Minnesota

Edge Books are published by Capstone Press,
151 Good Counsel Drive, P.O. Box 669, Mankato, Minnesota 56002.
www.capstonepress.com

Library of Congress Cataloging-in-Publication Data
Schaefer, A. R. (Adam Richard), 1976–
    Richard Petty / by A. R. Schaefer.
    p. cm.—(Edge Books. NASCAR racing)
    Includes bibliographical references and index.
    ISBN-13 978-0-7368-4378-2 (hardcover)
    ISBN-10 0-7368-4378-7 (hardcover)
    1. Petty, Richard—Juvenile literature. 2. Stock car drivers—United States—
Biography—Juvenile literature. 3. NASCAR (Association)—Juvenile literature. I. Title.
II. Series.
GV1032.P47S35 2007
796.72'092—dc22   2004028607

Summary: Discusses the life of legendary NASCAR driver Richard Petty, including his
    early career, records, and famous races.

Editorial Credits
Erika L. Shores, editor; Jason Knudson, set designer; Patrick D. Dentinger,
    book designer; Jo Miller, photo researcher

Photo Credits
AP/Wide World Photos, 6, 11, 13; Chris O'Meara, 8; Lynne Sladky, cover (foreground)
Corbis/Bettmann, 5, 17, 19, 28
Getty Images Inc./Time Life Pictures/Bob Peterson, 20
SportsChrome Inc., 23; Greg Crisp, cover (background)
Wire Image/Kevin Kane, 24, 27

Table of Contents

CHAPTER 1

Unforgettable Finish

The Daytona 500 is the biggest NASCAR race of the year. People call it "The Great American Race." In 1976, the Daytona 500 was more than great. Fans consider it one of the most exciting NASCAR races ever.

Richard Petty's Dodge and David Pearson's Mercury were the fastest two cars on the track. They fought each other for the lead throughout the race.

By the final lap, Richard and Pearson had outrun the other drivers by more than a lap. Richard led through the first two turns. On the backstretch, Pearson managed to get around him.

Learn about:

→ 1976 Daytona 500

→ Final lap wreck

→ "The King"

A crash into a wall wrecked Richard's car.

Richard wouldn't give up that easily. He came back to pass Pearson in turn 3. Angry, Pearson hit Richard's bumper to make him move out of the way. Both drivers lost control. Pearson and Richard slammed into the wall. Then Richard spun into the infield grass.

When Richard's car stopped, he was only 20 yards (18 meters) from the finish line. But he couldn't get his car started again. He watched as Pearson drove past him at about 20 miles (32 kilometers) per hour. Pearson's car was a mess and his tires were blown, but he crossed the finish line first.

Although Richard lost the 1976 Daytona 500, it's known as one of his greatest races. He went on to win the Daytona 500 seven times.

Richard Petty

Richard Petty is one of the best stock car drivers in NASCAR history. He raced in NASCAR from 1958 to 1992. He won 200 races. He won both the Daytona 500 and the NASCAR championship seven times.

NASCAR legend Richard Petty had 200 career wins.

Richard's success on the track was important to his image. But his personality off the track was just as important. Early in his career, Richard earned a reputation for treating people well. People often asked for his autograph. Richard never refused to give them one.

Richard was the dominant driver in NASCAR racing during the 1960s and 1970s. He finished in the top ten in points for 19 straight seasons. His performance and likable personality earned him the nickname "The King."

"Racing is where you run up there and beat on someone, and you get by them and then you go on to the next guy."
—Richard Petty, 2003, speedtv.com

CHAPTER 2

Introduction to Racing

Richard always loved watching cars race. He came from a family of race car drivers. But he had to wait to get his chance to compete.

Racing Beginnings

Richard was born on July 2, 1937. He grew up in Level Cross, North Carolina. People raced their cars on the flat, dirt country roads near this small town. One of the best of these racers was Lee Petty, Richard's father.

For years, Lee made money by betting other drivers that he could beat them on the country roads. He became widely known as a great driver.

NASCAR was formed in December 1947. On June 19, 1949, Lee Petty competed in the first official NASCAR stock car race, in Charlotte, North Carolina. Lee finished second in the points standings the first year. Encouraged by his success, Lee decided to continue racing in 1950.

Lee Petty (middle) taught Richard (right) and his brother Maurice (left) to love racing.

Learn about:

→ NASCAR's early days

→ Lee Petty

→ The first win

Famous Father

Before the 1950 season, Lee made another big decision. He wanted Richard to go with him to races and help the mechanics work on the car. At age 12, Richard was excited about the offer.

Richard went with Lee all over the country. He later said it was the most fun he ever had. He helped his father work on the blue number 42 Plymouth. They painted the car themselves. They called the color Petty blue.

When he was 18, Richard asked his father if he could race in NASCAR. Lee told his son that he had to wait until he was 21. Richard didn't say a word about it for three years. He continued to work for his father. He also raced his car on the country roads of North Carolina when he got the chance.

"I probably run harder when I'm in tenth place than I do when I'm leading . . . because I don't like to be in tenth place, and I do everything I can to improve my situation."
—Richard Petty, *King Richard I*

The Early Days

On the day after his 21st birthday, Richard asked his father again. This time, Lee pointed to the Petty team's second car, a 1957 Oldsmobile convertible. The car was Richard's to drive. Richard began racing it in NASCAR's convertible series.

Richard's first race was in Columbia, South Carolina, in 1958. He finished sixth. He drove in nine races that year and didn't finish in the top ten again. The next year, he felt more confident. He had more experience driving the car.

Richard's father, Lee, drove in early NASCAR stock races.

Early in 1959, Richard and his father were driving in the same race. Richard raced well all day. He wasn't surprised when the track official waved the checkered flag over his car.

Richard was excited to win in only his second season. He had driven into the winner's circle when a track official quickly came over and apologized. Another driver had protested. Richard was one lap short of winning the race. Officials had waved the checkered flag one lap too soon. Richard asked who had protested the finish. His father Lee had protested and was declared the winner.

Richard didn't wait much longer for his first win. It came in Columbia, South Carolina, in July 1959, where he had started his racing career a year earlier.

Career Statistics

Richard Petty

Year	Starts	Wins	Top 5s	Top 10s	Winnings
1958	9	0	0	1	$760
1959	21	0	6	9	$8,110
1960	40	3	16	30	$41,873
1961	42	2	18	23	$25,239
1962	52	8	32	39	$60,763
1963	54	14	30	39	$55,964
1964	61	9	37	43	$114,771
1965	14	4	10	10	$16,450
1966	39	8	20	22	$94,666
1967	48	27	38	40	$150,196
1968	49	16	31	35	$99,535
1969	50	10	31	38	$129,906
1970	40	18	27	31	$151,124
1971	46	21	38	41	$351,071
1972	31	8	25	28	$339,405
1973	28	6	15	17	$234,389
1974	30	10	22	23	$432,019
1975	30	13	21	24	$481,751
1976	30	3	19	22	$374,806
1977	30	5	20	23	$406,608
1978	30	0	11	17	$242,273
1979	31	5	23	27	$561,933
1980	31	2	15	19	$397,317
1981	31	3	12	16	$396,072
1982	30	0	9	16	$465,793
1983	30	3	9	21	$508,884
1984	30	2	5	13	$257,932
1985	28	0	1	13	$306,142
1986	29	0	4	11	$280,656
1987	29	0	9	14	$445,227
1988	29	0	1	5	$190,155
1989	25	0	0	0	$133,050
1990	29	0	0	1	$169,465
1991	29	0	0	1	$268,035
1992	29	0	0	0	$348,870
Career	1,184	200	555	712	$8,541,210

CHAPTER 3

Becoming the Best

In 1960, several things happened to help make Richard a star. First, NASCAR ended the convertible series.

Richard started driving the more popular stock cars. NASCAR also started building superspeedways. Daytona International Speedway opened in 1959. Other big tracks opened in 1960 in Atlanta and Charlotte. These tracks held thousands of fans. These fans soon saw what Richard Petty could do with a race car.

Becoming a Star

In 1960, Richard had a good year. He won three races and finished in the top ten in 30 of 40 races. He also finished second in the point standings for the year. NASCAR fans began to notice him.

Richard's success as a driver began in 1960.

Learn about:

→ A changing sport

→ Richard's best year

→ New colors for 43

Richard also finished second in the points in 1962 and 1963. During those two years, he won 22 races, but it wasn't enough.

Finally, in 1964, Petty started the season by winning the Daytona 500 and didn't look back. He won his first points championship that year. Richard Petty fans were now cheering for a champion.

Amazing Year

By 1967, Richard was one of the most popular NASCAR drivers. The season started out slowly for him. He blew an engine with five laps to go in the Daytona 500. He won a race in March, but nothing prepared people for what happened next.

Richard won an impressive four races in April. He was only just beginning. He flew past the competition, winning five more in July. He had six victories in September. At one point, he won 10 races in a row.

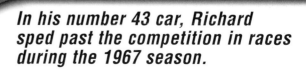
In his number 43 car, Richard sped past the competition in races during the 1967 season.

Until 1971, Richard's car was painted blue.

Richard won 27 out of 48 races that year. Only a few racers have won 27 races in their entire careers. He also won his second points championship. Richard's wins made for the most impressive season in NASCAR history. No driver has yet to top Richard Petty's 1967 season.

The Petty Car

In 1971, Richard had another great season. He won 21 races, including the Daytona 500, and a third points championship. When the season was over, Richard needed to find a new sponsor. STP was interested. The fuel and oil product company offered him a large contract. But they wanted him to paint his car red. The Petty cars that ran in NASCAR had always been Petty blue. Richard said he wouldn't drive a red car for any amount of money. Finally, the two sides came to an agreement. They painted the car red and blue.

CHAPTER 4

All-Time Great

Richard's success continued in his red and blue car. He won more races and more points championships. Many fans think he had the best stock car career ever.

An Amazing Career

In 1992, Richard retired. He won 200 NASCAR races. He won seven points championships and seven Daytona 500s. He finished in the top five in almost half of all the races that he ran. He won more than $8.5 million in his career. His 200 career wins and 10 wins in a row will probably never be broken.

STP sponsored Richard's car from 1971 until he retired in 1992.

Learn about:

→ Dominating driver

→ Record-breaking career

→ Helping kids

Richard made time to sign autographs for his many fans.

Richard saw the birth and growth of NASCAR. He was in Charlotte with Lee in 1949 for the first NASCAR stock car race. His win at Daytona in 1979 was the first NASCAR race to be completely televised live. President Ronald Reagan was at Daytona to congratulate Richard when he earned his 200th win.

Through all of his victories, Richard was humble and thankful to his fans. By the time he retired in 1992, the sport was popular across the country. Richard's skill and personality were a big part of that success.

The Petty Family

Richard and the Petty family have always been involved in NASCAR. Richard, his father, and Richard's brother, Maurice, raced on the same tracks for one season in the 1960s. Richard's son, Kyle, started racing in the 1970s. He has eight NASCAR wins.

In the late 1990s, Kyle's son, Adam, started racing. Adam raced in the Busch Series. In 2000, Adam was killed in a crash while practicing at a speedway in New Hampshire. He was only 19.

In 2004, Kyle, his wife Pattie, and Richard and his wife Lynda, opened a camp for kids with serious illnesses. Adam Petty had dreamed of starting a camp for sick children.

The Pettys' Victory Junction Gang Camp was built in Adam's memory. Children with serious diseases go to the NASCAR-themed camp to fish, swim, play sports, and build model race cars. Richard donated the land for the camp and visits often. He always makes sure to meet the campers and sign autographs.

"Racing was our destiny. Adam was a part of that."
—Richard Petty, 6-28-04, People

Actor Paul Newman joined Richard during the grand opening of the Victory Junction Gang Camp.

Career Highlights

1958 Richard drives in his first NASCAR race in an Oldsmobile convertible in Columbia, South Carolina.

1959 Richard wins his first NASCAR race at Columbia.

1964 Richard wins his first Daytona 500 and first NASCAR points championship.

1967 Richard wins a record 27 races and his second points championship.

1971 Richard wins 21 races and another points championship. After the season, he agrees with STP to create the well-known red and blue number 43 car.

1979 Richard wins his seventh and final NASCAR points championship.

1981 Richard wins his seventh Daytona 500.

1984 Richard wins his 200th race at Daytona.

1992 Richard retires after 35 years, 1,184 races, and 200 wins.

Glossary

convertible (kuhn-VUR-tuh-buhl)—a car with a top that can be put down or removed

declare (di-KLAIR)—to say something firmly

dominant (DOM-uh-nuhnt)—the most powerful member of a group

experience (ek-SPIHR-ee-uhnss)—the knowledge and skill a person gains by doing something

personality (pur-suh-NAL-uh-tee)—the qualities and traits that makes one person different from another

protest (pro-TEST)—to object to something publicly

reputation (rep-yuh-TAY-shuhn)—a person's worth or character, as judged by other people

Read More

Stewart, Mark. *The Pettys: Triumphs & Tragedies of Auto Racing's First Family.* Brookfield, Conn.: Millbrook Press, 2001.

Teitelbaum, Michael. *Richard Petty, "The King."* The World of NASCAR. Excelsior, Minn.: Tradition Books, 2003.

Internet Sites

FactHound offers a safe, fun way to find Internet sites related to this book. All of the sites on FactHound have been researched by our staff.

Here's how:

1. Visit *www.facthound.com*

2. Choose your grade level.

3. Type in this book ID **0736843787** for age-appropriate sites. You may also browse subjects by clicking on letters, or by clicking on pictures and words.

4. Click on the **Fetch It** button.

FactHound will fetch the best sites for you!

Index